# EROTIKA HOT STORIES - Part 2:

from the depth of the woman's mysterious soul overwhelmed with passionate desires

for men

and

for curious women

by

*Diane Rausch*

EROTIKA HOT STORIES - Part 2:
Overwhelmed with Passionate Desires

# Stories

# Hooligan is Having Sex in the Bathroom While her friend is Unsuspicious in the Room

## Hooligan's Hard Core Sex

Sorry, some "civil" interruptions there, in my story, but I'll get you aroused well finally, as you love it. A little sweet torture before relaxing finishing is good anyway, right?

I have read my Sex Word Picture of January 7, that I sent you and I got horribly aroused.

She (Laura) is sitting here bugging me with her pictures. She does not know computers as good so I have to help her and teach her.

OK. I showed her what she asked, and then I made her busy with FaceBook, because I am very horny, I need my sweet, delicious privacy, that I want to share with you.

I am saying to her, "Are you fine? I'll go to the bathroom."

That's a little place I can have my privacy, my sweet, delicious, satisfying, brain knocking from pleasure session of sex.

It is very weird how this lust thing works. I thought I am fine until I will come home next Friday, but I went to the folder to check my Sexy Note to you and here I am - aroused so strongly.

So, no big deal. I have to go and satisfy myself. You know, it is a physical thing, an animal thing. Just like an animal. It is a sudden call of the body.

Now, in the tiny bathroom of this little rental foreign country apartment, I do not have place to lie down. So, I have to do it sitting. However, I am inventive and creative! I want to act on my lust. I am so eager to act on my sweet sexy desire. I want the orgasm. My mind thinks about the sweet orgasm and relief. I am like a hungry animal on the hunt. In addition, I am also excited because I know I will tell you later my story and I will arouse you too. I love it. I love to get you hard. Maybe you will take your cream and do yourself after reading me, or simultaneously, when reading me. If you do that, that means we had sex together - I did myself, you were reading how I was doing myself, you were aroused and did yourself. The two minds were thinking about each other and sex. How exciting and beautiful! And it brings a physical and emotional relief, too.

Let's start, my Beloved.

I am taking off my cute tiny lacy bikini. I love my lacy bikinis! I have them all colors, and styles, and cuts. I look so cute in them. My pussy looks so adorable in them. If to sit in front of the mirror with my legs spread, and open the bikini on the pussy, moving it aside, my beautiful pink pussy lips will be right there. Arousing!

Pussy looking out of the lacy bikini! Delicious sight!

How often I was turned on just looking at myself in the mirror! How often I had to run to the bathroom and do myself on that arousal! I think it is very funny that I am aroused by my own body. Well, at least I do know exactly how arousing it is for a man!

Now, I am spreading the towel on the floor of a tiny room and sitting on it.

I am closing my eyes and opening my legs. I am spreading my beautiful long legs wide apart, as the space

9

permits, a little bit bending them in the knees. I am so horny, I am dying how I want to finish! I want to come, to cum beautifully. Only I will not be able to moan aloud, since the friend is in the room, behind the door.

I am imagining all sexy pictures I saw lately on TV, when by mistake we had the Playboy once, for a few days, right there, on our TV. I did not tell you then, but when I discovered the channel on TV, I watched it a few times, and then I did myself, I fucked myself sometimes when you were busy, or sleeping.

Now, also, I am imagining my open pussy. I saw it in the

mirror door of the closet in my room when I lived in my room in the Laguna house.

The sofa was standing in front of that big mirror because my room was rather small. I remember I was looking at my open pink pussy, with cute open lips, and I was thinking like this:

"I am never going to have a man who will lick me. And I love to be licked very much. It's the only way I can finish with a man. And this is a cute piece of a shaven cute pink pussy. I will live my life like a nun, because I will never have sex anymore. I am a married woman, and this is my life."

Also, in that room, when I was doing myself occasionally, at night, I was always thinking that I am a nun in the monastery. And all these prohibited sweet sexy thoughts about a man licking me.

Then I had a dream one night, and I wrote a story in my language after I woke up. The story was about the man I was deeply in love with. I felt that deep love through all the dream. It was unbelievably sweet feeling. When I woke up after that dream, I thought, "How strange that I even do not know to whom to attach that deep feeling of love; I was not even sure what time of my life

12

was in that story-dream, but the feeling was that the man was not English-speaking because the other feeling was that the story took place in my city. The city I was born in is one of the most beautiful cities in Europe.

OK. I think I got distracted now telling about my dream.

Now I want to finish telling about my doing myself today in the bathroom, since the lust was unbearable.

So, I will continue. When you read me, I hope, now, or after you can do yourself and finish well, like I just did.

It is just a simple relief of the combination of the intellectual and physical tension that our bodies experience from time to time. Of course, the more sensual is the person, the bigger is the fantasies, the more sexual triggering the person's mind will desire to experience.

I guess, I am a sensual person then. I think I like that. I think it's good when it is in a beautifully smart and decent frame - all the thing - thinking and acting on it. It's psychology. As my friend Laura said to somebody about me recently here, I don't remember, to whom, we are making many friends here,

14

so she said, laughing, "She is sexy, and she likes to look sexy!" And she laughed.

That's very true. I love the looks on me when I walk. They excite me. I imagine very well how a man get excited when he looks at an attractive female.

Here, in Europe, I am like a fish in the water. They are very fashionable here. In USA I forgot about it a little bit. Here, in this magnificent historical city, there are a lot of absolutely talented fruits of human hands (architecture and sculpture and paintings), and human expression of beauty - musicians, and a beautiful

15

young woman singer was singing once. Absolutely incomparable voice she had, and I, knowledgeable about languages could not tell was she French or other - her Spanish was perfect too.

When she was singing "Je t'aime" in French, she was looking at the accordion-player. I think she did not love him, but she wanted to have his support while opening her heart in front of the bunch of tourists at one of the picturesque, historical squares. She wanted the support of her friend when her soul was open. You cannot open your heart and look at the faceless multi-lingual crowd.

16

You have to have support. The beloved man's responding to that feeling would be the perfect support.

Sorry! I again slipped to some "city pictures", that I am observing here every day. I have many of them. When I come home, I want to write a book about my impressions of the city culture.

OK.

Let's come back to my sexy picture.

So, I am sitting on the towel, in the bathroom, with my legs spread, my eyes closed, and I am imagining sexy pictures, and the picture of my wet pussy, and I am fondling my pussy, I am doing myself, and doing myself, tenderly, and vigorously, at the same time.

My wet finger goes vertically, and horizontally, with circling movements. Insistently, and tenderly, and strongly, it is moving and moving, it is fucking my pussy. Oh, how sweet! The finger is wet because the wetness of the pussy has already been there since I took off my panties and sat in a position to have sex with myself.

I also lick my finger, from time to time. It's

delicious. My pussy is delicious. It tastes a little lemony. It is so sweet and good. It feels wonderfully exciting, when you are acting on the strong lust, desire, when you are very horny. You think that you can never have enough of it, you are enjoying yourself sinking in this pleasant thinking and acting on your beautiful sex organ: the unique source of a huge pleasure.

So I was fucking and fucking myself for about 5-6 minutes. I am continuing fondling myself with the finger, my pussy pink juicy beautiful aroused lips are open, the entrance to the tunnel of pleasure, my beautiful vagina, is very narrow and nice. I do not go there. The excitement is so big, that I even do not have to go there. I can do everything on the surface of my pussy.

Ah yes, it is not comfortable here anyway to relax in a conventional, as one can relax when they are lying on the bed.

But my desire to finish is so strong that I have a big confidence that I will finish soon. The feeling is like hunting. Impatience to finish, and, simultaneously, the patience to do the work well, in order to finish well, to have that nice cum, explosion, and relief of the tension created by desire and fucking hard.

It is a circle. A sexual circle of thinking. The action is absolutely pleasant. The expectation of the finishing, of the coming, of the wonderful orgasm, is absolutely exciting and pleasant. I go faster, and faster, my pussy is so wet, that there are even the little sounds of doing myself. They are like wet, some splashy sounds. The pussy has to be very wet to finish. Wet like from your tongue, when you lick me. Juice all over. Delicious pussy juice. The mature fruit of life. Then, all wet, it can finish in the wet happiness.

I know she is at computer, and she cannot hear me. So I go faster and faster, my heart is pounding, my eyes are closed, and I imagine you are fucking me, and licking me at the same time. I know it is physically impossible, but that is not important, I finish on that fantasy. My fantasy now is licking and fucking at the same time. What I could never do in real life, I can do easily fantasizing. Your tongue is licking me, licking my Clit, and your cock is fucking me in the pussy. Wow! It's coming, I am fucked so deliciously, the clit, and tunnel, the clit and tunnel, it's overwhelming!...

I am coming, I am coming strongly and sweetly. It lasts about a few seconds. The flight to paradise and unconsciousness about everything that is worldly lasts about a few seconds. What a flight! A flight to paradise and back to sinful earth.

It is such a beautiful relief! When I am coming, it seems, that every time I keep wondering: I cannot believe how short is the moment. I cannot believe how beautiful is the moment and how strong it is and how fast it is over.

The glorious sexual culmination.

If you were with me, you would eat my cum, and I would eat yours. And we would be completely happy, like a pair of lions, big cats, who just ate the big food, a prey animal, plenty of meat. We are full beautiful big cats.

I hope you can finish on this visual picture, sooner or later, or on my first picture, I sent you before, my beloved Baby.

You do not have to tell me what you are doing with yourself when you read me, or if you are not doing it. I have the feeling that because I am a woman, I can tell everything more openly. Women can tell everything to each other, but men are more reserved.

I love the quiet and reserved man who loves me. I know he loves me and wants to fuck me like crazy. It is my Baby.

## Sex Without Warming Up: Be Ready

I love you so much, my Beloved, I want you so much! I want to fuck you hard.

I want to suck your cock. I want to take your cock to fondle it with my tongue, with my hands, with my fingers. I want to caress your cock; I want to love you so much.

I thought how hard you could fuck me somewhere where we meet, and there would not be a regular bed, but we are dying to fuck. We are dying of love to each other and we want each other like crazy, and you take me standing, and

26

I lift my leg trying to help you. I want to sit myself on your stiff, hard cock that is standing like a soldier.

That is what I say about your cock - it is like a soldier on guard. I think you love that. You love your cock hard, and you love me loving it hard. You love my excitement.

I suck your cock very eagerly and tenderly, and then I put it inside me, in my pink pussy, a sweet narrow tunnel of paradisiacal pleasure. And you will caress my breasts.

You love my breasts. They are round, beautiful and nice, and they want to be caressed by your tender hands.

27

And I love your caressing of my pussy, when it is all wet inside. I love when you open it with your tender fingers, I love when you touch my rosy lips, they are thick and meaty, and horny, they are waiting for your caress.

I love when you touch my pussy, and your cock is hard, and you touch and fondle my open pussy and my wet lips. It is juicy, it is Juicy Pussy, and it is so eager for your sex.

My Pussy wants your hard tender wet tongue and your lips a lot; it wants to be caressed; it wants to finish; it wants to come with juicy cum; as I eat your good big portion of sperm; and you are releasing the tension from your mind together with your shot of fresh sperm; and you are flying for a second to the universe.

You are dying how you want our strong orgasmic explosions when making love to your sweet woman, your Baby, your Diane. Oh, how sweet is love! How good that both our hearts are trembling with love. Our hearts, minds, and bodies represent now one desire - our sweet sex. How hard and fast I want to fuck you! How eager I am to spread my legs for you! I want you to fuck me so many times, over and over again, with your cock, into my pussy.

Now I am sitting on you and jumping eagerly, fucking and fucking you, I cannot have enough of it.

Oh, lick me again! Open my legs very wide, spread them, open them! They are eager to feel the caress of your gentle and strong tongue licking my juicy sweet pussy.

Oh, how tasty! Oh, how delicious! I am dying from pleasure! I love you licking me. When you are licking me, I think, that you are fucking me with your tongue, like a cock fucks pussy, your tongue is a cock now, and it is fucking my pussy.

It is much smaller than the cock, but it is much more flexible. It can suck, and lick, and go around. The brave soldier cock can only fuck. Two of them are a huge power and source of pleasure.

I love how cute you speak. I love your accent. It is so sexy. And your tongue is so able and sexy. It speaks so cute, and it licks so excitingly.

Your tongue is a little hard flexible cock now. It goes along the lips and around the sweet little hole, and it sticks inside, as a busy little bee on the flower.

Your lips suck on my clit and my pussy so sweetly! I am

dying how I love your kissing and sucking of my pink eager pussy. I feel I can finish now.

I am becoming tenser, I want to finish. The moment is coming. The moment of cumming is coming! Lick me, lick me, my Baby, fuck me sweet and hard from behind! How good you are fucking me from behind; I feel your cock deep inside my sweet tunnel, going fast in and out. What pleasure!

Pull out your big cock from me now, turn me quickly on my back, and lick me again, and fuck me again, I want to feel simultaneously your cock and your tongue, I am unbearably greedy for your desire. Fuck me well, and, please, finish yourself. Explode while you are licking me. Explode from your heart feeling of love to me. Explode from your feeling of my huge desire to cum from your tongue.

I can suck your cock simultaneously with your licking my pussy. I cannot finish from sixty-nine position though. It is just an enormous intellectual pleasure that we are sucking each other's organs of highest physical pleasure.

Now fuck me again. Good, hard. Look in my eyes. I love you to death. I cannot believe I love you so much, and you fuck me so good.

I will swallow your cum. And I will get it all over my breasts and my pussy. I guess I have to choose how I want it now. I love you so much, fuck me more, my Baby, and let me fuck you.

Let me take your cock once more, tenderly, very deep in my mouth, to my throat. Go faster, my Beloved, so I know you are fucking me in the throat as you are fucking me in the pussy's sweet wet hole.

I love you fucking me. I love to give you sex. I love to finish and to give you sex. I love you to use me for sex. I love to be used by you for

34

sex. I want you so much: I am dying, how good it is.

Let's fuck each other like crazy. It is so beautiful! My Beloved! We are so in love, and we love to fuck each other so much!

Lets finish together. Finish, finish, my Beloved, moan, and lick me, as you are finishing, and I start finishing, too. Eat it! Eat my cum! I love you so much!

## Sex For My Baby

My Baby, let me tell you what I want to do with you.

I want to unzip your jeans and get your hard warm cock out of there, and I want to fondle your cock with my fingers - to run it with the tips of my fingers very tenderly like playing the flute. Oh, that will be a beautiful melody of your flute, a beautiful song of my loving heart.

Your cock is my favorite flute - your beautiful cock is my favorite toy and a musical instrument. I know how you like when I touch you at the shaft, along the shaft of your cock.

The shaft. It is very pleasant to touch you there, playing my fingers, as I am playing the flute.

As I am writing, my pussy starts squeezing from excitement, because I am thinking about our fucking.

I yesterday told Laura, that we fucked with you outside of the house, in the backyard. She said, "Well, it's your backyard, you can do whatever you want there".

My Baby, I remember just the general scenes of our fucking, the strongest scenes that are in my memory.

I'll tell you what they are.

One is in Washington DC, in your mom's bedroom.

One is on the floor in your Beach house living room.

In Las Vegas, when you had to fly out of there quickly for your business, and I stayed there with Laura and her husband, I was dying for you.

OK.

While memories are sweet, the reality calls us.

Let's get back to our sucking, fucking, and licking business.

I am going to suck your cock now. I know how you like to slide it very deep into my throat. Then you like to take it out for about three little times, then again deep in the throat.

Fuck me, my baby, fuck me in the mouth. My lips are squeezing your pink cock tightly and pleasantly. I am licking my Baby's cock. I am running my pink tongue from the bottom to the head of your cute cock. Then I take it in the wet mouth. I suck on it tenderly. Then I take it out and quickly turn with my back to you, and I am standing now a doggie style, and you see my cute pussy, and you start fucking me like this. Your slippery cock goes easily into my eager pussy after my mouth's sweet sucking treatment.

I love you fucking me like this, a doggie style. It is so delicious. As I am writing, my Pussy is squeezing, all tight from the excitement, because I am visualizing the image.

You are fucking me, fucking me, licking me, licking me, and then you are ready to explode with your sweet cum. You want to explode into my mouth this time, so

40

you are exploding into my mouth very big and strong. Very big and strong. Shoot it! The ground is slipping away from under you. You are flying into Universe for a second. You are flying through the roof into the Universe for a second. It is the most beautiful excitement in the world, to satisfy your lust with your horny Baby.

I love you, my Baby.

Your Diane.

# A Letter to my Cowboy:
# Pink Lips Opened

I was doing my writing project, but inside my mind were you. So, I opened a clean page and had sex with my beloved. It's much more entertaining even than my favorite literary pieces in the languages that I love. Nothing compares with making love to my Cowboy. It's intense and unforgettable. It keeps me going. It's playing with my brain. It adds a beautiful sense to my life.

Here it is. Sit tight, my beloved, and enjoy, as I enjoyed it when I was writing it and rereading it.

I have small tight ears, very cute. May be you didn't know or never paid attention. Now you know. My ears are my pride. I hate big ears in other women. Some women even do not have a decent esthetical taste to close their big ears with hair. What a man thinks when he caresses big ears, that they are elephant's ears? (Unless the man depends on that elephant: in that case, he makes himself not notice).

I know what you think when you caress my cute ears:

that you are caressing the small ears of a beautiful, very sexual woman, the woman with a perfect sense for beauty.

We are sitting on the sofa, and hugging, getting excited. Now you got with the tongue close to my ear, whispering about your love. It feels very ticklish and very arousing. It is ticklish and arousing for my heart, for my muscles, and for my soul. I love you. And I am expecting to have a good sex from my Beloved now. The ear communicates with my pussy, for some reason. Your tongue is wet, the pussy now thinks that hers is the next turn after the ear. My pussy is creaming about your tongue. It is jealous that the tongue is doing ear.

You are sucking the soft tip of the ear and then you go with the tip of the tongue inside the ear. It is very exciting. With your hands, simultaneously, you are fondling the inside of my legs, gently trying to spread them apart. I pretend that I finally "give up", trying to fake some resistance (to turn you on stronger), and I let your hand to fondle my pussy. Your tongue is still doing my ear.

Your hand is fondling my pussy, that is getting wetter

and more slippery by the moment, and your tongue is licking and sucking my ear. An unbearably arousing exciting moment!

Then you start caressing my beautiful round breasts with light pink innocent nipples. I love when you take my breast in your hand - it fits there perfectly. My breasts are of average very good size. I have a perfectly proportional figure. I have always been an eye turner having the perfect sense of style and color too. I am a pleaser of any eye, not only man's. Women would come up to me in public places and compliment me.

46

Sorry, I stepped away from our important business. I am a simple woman after all: I like sharing.

Now you are crawling down to the floor rug in front of me trying to get between my legs. You are looking at the pussy. With your beautiful grayish greenish eyes. You are feeding your physical desire with the esthetical feeling of natural woman's beauty. My breasts are natural; my buttocks are cute and natural. My muscle tone is just naturally perfect (I love to fuck and get pleasure, exciting my meticulous mind, for the exercise, with my man all my life), so my muscle

47

tone is not too manly, and not overly soft.

I remember looking at my pussy in the mirror. It was in my room of the Laguna house, where there is a mirrored closet door opposite the bed where I was sleeping at that time. I saw the pink pussy. I know it is very cute: right there, inside the wide-open long, smooth legs.

The pussy is open now, because I am opening it with my hands. My nail polish is a very light pearl pink color. The pearly very light pink nails look very cute, they are opening the exciting live pink treasure for you, and for us:

to have a variety of pleasurable sensations.

It's open and waiting. You are already familiar with a little tiny funny thing on the top. You call it a funny name "Clit".

It likes to be licked and sucked on. It is a trigger to go to paradise, when I am having orgasm, if you are able to measure correctly the monotonous rhythm of the movements of the tip of your tongue. The movements of your tongue should be around it, and sucking it, and licking the whole thing.

You are totally into it. Because it is delicious. Maybe

before you were not into it.
Now you are. It is the source
of pleasure for the both
minds. You are tenderly
sucking the little thing with
your attractive manly lips.
You are going down with your
tongue to the entrance to let
it know once more that it's
not forgotten.

The entrance of my pussy
appreciates the care. I am
moaning, "Ah, Cowboy, je
t'aime, te amo, I love you".

In my language it feels
very strong, because it is the
prevailing language I grew up
with. We do not use these
words if we do not feel it. I
love you licking me and I love
you for you.

I am relaxed and flying in the skies. My Cowboy is licking me. I raise my hips a little from the sofa to get you better, to feel you better.

I am coming now. I am moaning louder because the pleasure is impossible to sustain. You are licking me until I finish to finish, until I finish to come. To come with a cum - oh, juicy! You are licking and sucking, and eating my juice. You are very happy that I just came. You feel like a boy who just got his favorite toy.

My coming, my beautiful orgasm, is lasting about a minute or so. I need you right away on the top of me. I've missed you, while you were far from me, licking my pussy. I missed my man. I wanted my pussy licked, but I was missing you, too. You are going to fuck me good now. I am sitting here and moving around on my chair, while writing, my muscles on which I am sitting are contracting - I feel how you are entering me, from the top, sinking between my widely spread legs, in that open, just finished with cum, my narrow tunnel. It is a total knock out: you entered me after I just came. I am kissing you. We are one body now. I still need to feel fucking: just licking is not making the complete feeling of having my man. I need fucking in a quick succession after licking and coming - to feel a complete satisfaction.

You go deep, to the place where the juice just came from. You are going there with the top of your beautiful cock. Like a rocket into a special garage.

You are starting fucking me strongly, I am asking for it. I love to feel your strength. I have the feeling now that I am continuing finishing from your cock because you got there in time of opening, at the time when everything is opened after the good orgasm.

It is a wonderful feeling! Very complete and absolutely happy. I am done, but I want to feel your strength from behind. Besides, I like to move around a little. I have a beautiful figure, I always did. I love to give it to men. I now have had you for a few years. I love to give it to you. We are never tired to fuck and enjoy each other. What happiness!

You are turning me upside down with your strong warm tender hands and dragging me closer to your hard eager cock, my beloved cock that has not finished yet.

I am helping you back inside where you were two

seconds ago. We just changed positions. You are holding me with both hands by the waist and you are putting me on, on your cock. You are putting me on, like I am a piece of clothing. A piece of clothing, a beautiful woman, that has to cover your cock, the beautiful tender woman's body has to wrap around your cock tightly.

You are looking at my body from behind, at my thin waist, and round hips, and the perfect size buttocks. You are enjoying the picture. How delicious! You are fucking me so deliciously. In and out. In and out. In and out. I am bending my back lowering my belly down to the sofa, like a female-cat. I am moaning from pleasure. I am saying, "Oh, Baby, I love how you are fucking me! Fuck me more my Baby! I cannot have enough of you!"

I feel your beautiful thing, cock, is doing me from behind pushing in and going out so deliciously! It's a beautiful feeling of your strength from behind. I love it. I am getting exhausted. You are doing the last few movements and you are exploding in me. You are saying "My Diane, my love". I feel a ticklish feeling of your cum. It is very pleasant! It is almost like my orgasm, but much shorter, only for a second, at the moment when your cum shoots into my depth.

It feels good!

You are pulling your wet cock out of me and I am taking your nice wet cock with my hand and into my mouth: I am licking it dry. It's our love. It's nice and innocent. It's the most beautiful thing in the world.

My Cowboy. I can have you very often. I love to have you often. I know you are enjoying it too.

My Cowboy says when I am away from him, "My Angel, if you only knew how easily I relax fantasizing and dreaming of you.

The erotic visions I have with your wonderfully descriptive pictures are beautiful! Thank you for not being ashamed to tell me these things. There is nothing I would not do to please you, and everything you do or tell me pleases me.... to amazing heights! I think of such pleasure unburdened with shame or modesty.

Is it bad? Not between two mature people who are comfortable with themselves and each other, as we have become. It is these delicious thoughts that keep me longing for you. I think, "how can a woman who is equal to my intellectual thoughts as no other, be such a sensual, sexual creature as well?!". It is simply who you

are, my Delicious, Exotic
Beauty, My Love, My Diane".